VOLLEYBALL
ATTACKING TO WIN

ZACHARY A. KELLY

The Rourke Corporation, Inc.
Vero Beach, Florida 32964

PHOTO CREDITS:
All photos © Tony Gray

Illustration page 4 © East Coast Studios

PROJECT EDITORIAL SERVICES:
Harold Lockhelmer, Connie Denaburg

EDITORIAL SERVICES:
Penworthy Learning Systems

Library of Congress Cataloging-in-Publication Data

Kelly, Zachary A., 1970-
    Volleyball—attacking to win / Zachary A. Kelly.
        p. cm. — (Volleyball)
    Includes index.
    Summary: Discusses various offensive and defensive techniques in volleyball, including passing, attacking, and having specialized players in particular positions.
    ISBN 0-86593-503-3
    1. Volleyball—Juvenile literature. [1. Volleyball.] I. Title II. Series:
Kelly, Zachary A., 1970- Volleyball.
QV1015.3.K44 1998
796.325—dc21   98–25927
                                                         CIP
                                                          AC

Printed in the USA

TABLE OF CONTENTS

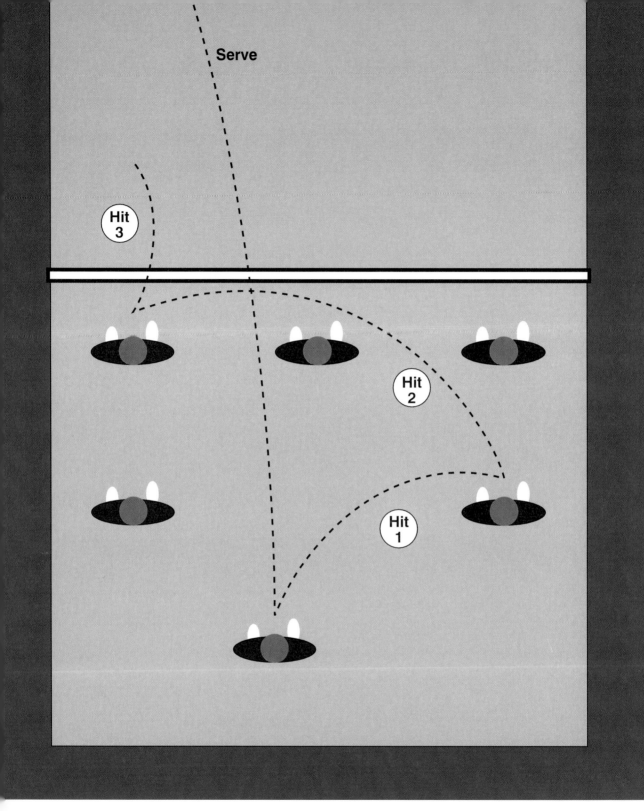

Diagram showing the bump (hit 1), set (hit 2), attack (hit 3.)

FROM DEFENSE TO OFFENSE

In some sports, it is clear who is playing offense and who is playing defense. The direction of the ball shows who is on offense in basketball and soccer. In football, the team playing offense possesses the ball. Players in these sports specialize in offense or defense to help their team win.

Volleyball is different. In this sport, both teams use offensive and defensive moves in every play. The key to winning is to turn the play from defense to offense. In volleyball, players may specialize in offensive or defensive moves, but every teammate plays both throughout a game.

In fact, most teams are taught that the only time you are on defense is while receiving a spike.

When volleyball players receive the ball, they try to use it against the other team. That requires three actions: The team keeps the ball from hitting the floor (pass or dig), gets control of it (**set**), and sends it over the net as a spike or an **attack**, so that it is hard for the other team to hit (dig). This technique of "**three-hits-and-over**" is the most common way that volleyball players move each play from defense to offense.

The Pass

The **pass** is the first part of three-hits-and-over. A good pass keeps the ball from hitting the floor and makes it easy for the next teammate to set it. The most common pass for this first hit is the **forearm pass**. If the player makes a good pass, the next player can choose where to set the second hit. The pass is the key to turning the play from defense to offense.

To perform a forearm pass, the players watch the ball as it comes over the net. If the play is a serve, or if the ball is coming at waist level or lower, the receiving player will use a forearm pass. First, the player approaches the ball with a series of short steps.

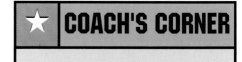

COACH'S CORNER

Imagine that you have a board across your forearms and hands as you practice passing and digging the ball. This will help you use your platform.

This player shifts to the left to dig the ball.

A good follow-through is important on a set.

Then the player stops, rounds the shoulders forward, and brings the palms of the hands together to make a platform for the ball. (Hands should be in light fists.) With knees bent and arms parallel to thighs, the player contacts the ball, and passes for the next player.

The Set

The second hit, when three hits are used, is a set. A set is an overhead pass that sets up the ball for the **attack** or **spike**. A good set makes it easy for the next player to use the ball offensively against the other team. A setter will use several kinds of sets, including back set, high set, quick or short set, and **jump set**. A setter watches the other team and works with the hitter to prepare the third hit.

★ DID YOU KNOW?

Who won the Gold Medal for volleyball in the 1996 Olympics? The Netherlands won the men's competition; Cuba, the women's event.

All sets have preparation in common. To begin a set, a player moves into a balanced position with the hands up, directly over the forehead in a triangle position. The hands are open, with the thumbs and index fingers making a triangle shape. The ball is passed to the attacker with a soft, quick press using all ten pads of your fingertips on the ball.

In a jump set, the setter jumps up to set the ball, and sets it while in the air. In any kind of set, though, the other team should not know what the setter will do with the ball until it is already moving to the attacker.

The Attack

An attack is the last of three hits a team uses to put the ball over the net. Since it is the final hit, the attack is always offensive. A good attack is difficult for the other team to dig. It may be a powerful hit, or it may be a surprise for the opposing players; but any good attack keeps the other team on defense.

Setting the ball for an attack during a tournament.

A good block is as important as a good attack.

A player can choose from several kinds of attacks to make an offensive hit. A **tip**, or **dink**, is a soft touch that sends the ball just over the net. If the opposing players are expecting a hard hit, the tip can throw them off. A **spike** is a powerful hit that sends the ball quickly to the other team's floor. Unless they are expecting it, this attack is a difficult technique for players to dig. A second version of a spike—a half or soft spike—is also a common attack. It is a combination of a tip approach and spike contact. As in the set, the attacks look the same until the last moment, so that the other team must guess what the hit will be.

THE PASS

A forearm pass is the key to moving from defense to offense. Players use it almost always as the first step of three-hits-and-over. Three situations in a play call for a forearm pass: 1. Serve-receive, 2. Free ball, and 3. digging a spike.

Since the forearm pass reduces spin and speed, the ball goes to the front court players with less force. This keeps them from having to slow the ball down themselves, and lets them place it for the attack.

If the ball is coming from waist height, a player will usually use a forearm pass. This pass uses a low- to medium-body position, allowing a player to hit the ball easily, even if it is very low. The pass gives a player stability and power to control the ball and begin an offensive play for the team.

How to Make a Forearm Pass

To prepare the forearm pass, move toward the ball quickly and stop. Keep your feet a little farther apart than the width of your shoulders. Your toes, hips, and shoulders should point in the direction you want the ball to go. Put your right foot slightly forward with your weight on the other foot. Keep your knees bent.

Round your shoulders forward to create a "hollow" chest, and bring your hands together in front of your body with the forearms up towards the ceiling and elbows slightly together. This creates the platform for your hit. Your thumbs should touch, and your wrists should face the target. Keep your eyes on the ball.

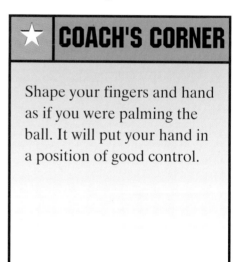

★ **COACH'S CORNER**

Shape your fingers and hand as if you were palming the ball. It will put your hand in a position of good control.

This player chose a dig instead of a forearm pass.

A good stance for a forearm pass or bump.

Contact the ball with both forearms just above the wrists. Shift your weight forward as you hit it. Keep your body behind the ball. You should let the ball rebound off your arms, not lift it or swing at it. The angle of your hit will determine the angle of the ball's path. The higher the platform the higher the ball; so aim your hit before, during, and after contact. Keep your eyes on the ball during the entire pass.

Improving Your Pass

A good pass takes the force of the ball at contact. To do this keep your body behind the ball and keep your arms parallel to (even with) your thighs. Hold your arms away from your body. With your legs staggered (apart, one in front of the other) and your arms directly in front of you, your body will take most of the force. Do not add force to the ball by swinging your arms. Simply receive the ball and let it rebound.

A good pass also directs the ball to a teammate. Since you do not want to add force to the ball, you cannot direct the ball with your arms. You must use your body and the angle of your arms at contact.

The angle of contact will determine how the ball rebounds. So watch the ball as it comes toward you and angle your arms for an accurate hit.

Who is the Passer?

When the ball comes over the net, one person on the team should move to receive it. To choose which player will do that, the team must watch the ball as it travels to their side. Back court players have priority in receiving the ball if they have a better chance of playing it in line with their body. Many balls arriving below waist level become the responsibility of back court players.

This back court player prepares to receive the ball while her teammates shift positions.

Keeping your elbows together when using a forearm pass gives
you better control.

Once the ball's path is clear, the player to receive it should call for it and move to receive. A player may say, "Mine," "I've got it," or "ball" to call for the ball. Even though it may seem simple, calling the ball is one of the most important parts of a passer's job. Calling the ball makes sure that only one player moves to receive the ball.

After a passer calls for the ball, the other players on the team should "open the passing lanes." All players not involved with the pass should move out of the way, facing the passer to be ready for the next hit, the set.

THE SET

A Setter's Job

A set is the second hit in three-hits-and-over. The set is an overhead pass that puts the ball near an attacker. An attacker then hits it over the net for the attack. A setter must watch the passer to see where the ball is coming from. Then he or she must watch the other team to know where to place the ball. A setter must place the ball accurately so that the attacker can play it with as much control as possible.

There are three kinds of sets that differ in where the setter places the ball. A setter tries to make all sets look alike until the ball is in the air, even if one set is very different.

A setter can do a high outside set that places the ball on the far side of the court. An attacker has to come to the ball in this set. In a quick set, a setter sets the ball one to three feet higher than the top of the net directly in front of him or her. A setter must get the ball to an attacker in a quick set, because the attacker approaches with a jump before attacking. In a back set, a setter sets the ball behind his or her head for an attack.

Making an Overhead Pass

The sets mentioned so far involve an overhead pass. To do an overhead pass, move to the ball quickly and get in a balanced position. Your toes, knees, and shoulders should face your target, which is the attacker. Your feet should be in a comfortable position with your weight evenly distributed. Knees, hips, and elbows should bend slightly, your hands above your head. Look through your fingers and keep your eyes on the ball.

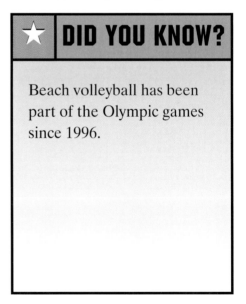

★ **DID YOU KNOW?**

Beach volleyball has been part of the Olympic games since 1996.

This player practices an overhand pass.

When tipping the ball, do not let it rest in your hands.

Contact the ball on the lower back side and let your hands move back slightly as they take the impact of the hit. Shift your weight forward and let your legs, hips, arms, and hands push the ball toward the target. Direct the ball to the height you want for the set. Aim it for the antennae for an outside set, or the spot on the floor where the attacker will be hitting. Focus on the ball!

Once the ball is in motion, follow through by extending your arms fully. Point your hands and hips toward the target as your weight moves forward; then move toward the set.

A back set pass is similar to a front set pass. The preparation is alike, and the contact is almost the same. The difference between the two passes involves just one part of the body—the hips. When the setter contacts the ball, he or she quickly thrusts the hips forward to make a back set. The arms extend straight over the head and the setter passes the ball up and back. The quicker the hips move, the farther back the pass will travel. As the back set is perfected, you should use more wrist to set the ball behind the setter. This will prevent your opponent from watching your body movements and guessing your back set.

 COACH'S CORNER

Make a diamond shape with your thumbs and forefingers and center the ball between them as you receive a high pass. It will improve your accuracy.

Jump Set and Setter Attack

Experienced volleyball players sometimes use two more skills—the jump set and **setter attack**. These advanced skills are useful only after a player is consistent in all other setting skills. A coach can help you decide when to begin using these techniques.

These players practice a jump set.

This player misses a block and goes for a jump set.

A jump set is similar to an overhead pass, except that the setter contacts the ball in the air. As the pass approaches, the setter jumps with the body upright to the net, hitting the ball just above his or her forehead. In a jump set, the setter can do a high outside pass, a quick pass, or even a back pass. By arching the back at the peak of the jump, the setter directs the ball back.

The setter attack is a surprise move for the other team. The setter can do this pass as a regular overhead pass or as a jump set. After the ball has passed one shoulder, the setter uses a quick snap of the wrist to send the ball over the net. The setter attack is hard to do.

THE ATTACK

An Attacker's Job

An attack is the last hit in the three-hits-and-over technique. This hit sends the ball over the net in a way that makes it difficult for the other team to receive it. It is the most offensive move in the play. Three basic attacks are used: the tip (or dink), the off-speed spike, and the hard-driven spike. When people hear the word "spike," they often think of the hard-driven spike. It is the fastest play in volleyball.

An attacker keeps several thoughts in mind when making an attack. First, an attacker makes sure the ball is not a free ball. A free ball is a forearm pass over the net to your opponent. If a team is not able to bump, set, or spike a ball as an offensive play, they give a "free ball." Easy to receive, a free ball puts the opponent on the offensive, with the possibility of scoring.

Second, an attacker watches the other team and looks for ways to keep them off balance. Changing the timing, angle, and kind of attack keeps the other team guessing. Third, an attacker watches for the other team's weaknesses and tries to take advantage of them to gain the offensive.

The Approach

The beginning of an attack is called the "**approach**." All three attacks begin the same way. Start the approach when the ball is at its highest point in the air. Go to the net using only three steps if possible. The last two steps are the most important. If you are right-handed, plant the heel of your right foot and bring your left foot slightly in front of it before jumping. (Left-handed players plant the left heel and so on.)

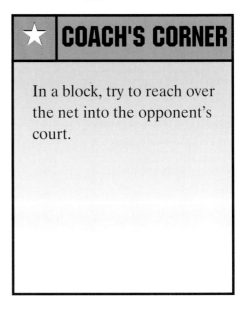

★ COACH'S CORNER

In a block, try to reach over the net into the opponent's court.

This player slams the ball for a high-speed attack.

This player shows good form for jumping to spike the ball.

As you plant your feet, swing both arms back behind you. Transfer your weight forward, swing your arms forward and up, and jump straight up into the air. Planting your feet and shifting your weight helps keep you moving straight up, instead of allowing you to drift toward the net in the air. Bring your hitting arm back with your elbow high. Your hand should be close to your ear. As you contact the ball, drop your non-hitting hand. Return to the floor with knees bent and eyes still on the ball. You need to reach up and contact the ball as high as possible above the net and slightly in front of you. Use your wrist to snap the ball down.

Tip, Off-Speed Spike, and Hard-Driven Spike

To do a tip (dink), approach the ball as in an attack situation. Extend your arm fully and contact the ball using the upper two finger joints of your hitting hand. You should be touching the lower back half of the ball. With little force, direct the ball over or around the other team's defense so that it drops over the net. This gentle attack often throws the other team off balance.

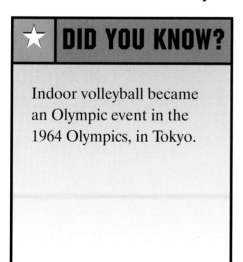

DID YOU KNOW?

Indoor volleyball became an Olympic event in the 1964 Olympics, in Tokyo.

For an **off-speed spike**, make contact with the ball when your arm is fully extended in front of your hitting shoulder. Use the heel of your hand to hit the ball on its lower back half. Snap your wrist and let your fingers roll over the top of the ball, giving it a fast-dropping topspin.

To do a **hard-driven spike**, contact the ball with a fully extended arm slightly in front of your hitting shoulder. Hit with the heel of your open hand on the back center of the ball. Snap your wrist forcefully with your hand over the top of the ball to send it quickly to the floor.

Switching quickly to a tip from a spike can confuse an opponent.

A quick set at the net catches the opponent off-guard.

Choosing Your Attack

For all attacks, keep the approach the same. Keep your eyes on the ball throughout your action, and choose a technique that will challenge the other team.

A tip is useful for changing the timing of your attack. After a few spikes, a tip can surprise the opposing team. A tip is also a very shallow attack. It travels only a short way over the other team's court before dropping. That is useful if the other team is in a deep-court formation.

An advantage of an off-speed spike is that it goes deep into the opponent's court, or to an area of the court that is open. An attacker doing an off-speed spike focuses on placing the ball in a weak area of the court. An off-speed spike is not as powerful as a hard-driven spike, but it gives an attacker more choices than a tip.

A hard-driven spike is the most powerful offensive weapon. Because a hard-driven spike moves quickly, the other team can dig it only if they are already in position for it, or can move quickly to it. A hard-driven spike is also the most difficult attack to perform.

SPECIALIZATION AND CALLING THE SHOT

Rotation in the game of volleyball makes it different from any other sport. Since the players must rotate one position every time their team earns a sideout, each player must learn six positions. That requires a lot of practice time, for each player and the whole team. Once a player has learned to play a certain position, he or she must learn to work in that position with the rest of the team. Formations, team plays, and offensive and defensive moves must all be relearned and practiced with each rotation.

To make rotation easier, many coaches specialize their players. When a team is specialized, each player learns only two positions, one in back court and one in front. Since back court players cannot block or spike in front of the attack line, it is important to distinguish the two halves of the court. Some teams keep a player on one side of the court, always on the right side or the left. Some teams specialize players by roles, such as setters and attackers. Many teams combine the ways that players specialize.

Setters and Attackers

Many teams divide their players into setters and attackers. The players learn the make up of their roles as well as how to defend the front and back court. A setter is a player who plans the offense of a team. He or she must be a good leader, a good athlete, and make good decisions under pressure. A setter must communicate well with his or her teammates to lead a team and direct attacks. Many coaches look for setters who can hit with either hand or are left-handed. Setters also need good peripheral vision (see to their right and left) to watch the other team. The setters are often thought of as the most skilled members of a team.

★ COACH'S CORNER

When you block, do not touch the net. Be aware of how fast you are moving and how close you are to the net. Pull your hands back quickly after the block.

Three players eye the ball as they practice overhand floaters.

This player's in the "ready" position to set the ball.

Coaches look for several traits in attackers, too. A player should jump well and be able to hit the ball with a lot of force to score points with an attack. An attacker also needs to show self-confidence on the court and not give up. Attackers also must watch the other team and counter its defense.

Middle Players

Setters often play the right front and right back positions. Power hitters (attackers) often play on the left side of the court. Left-handed players are most useful for the right side positions, since they allow a team to have power hitters on both sides of the court. Middle hitters also have important jobs in offensive plays.

Middle players should be aware of the entire court, so they need good peripheral vision. They look for the weak spots all over their court and move quickly to cover them before the other team can take advantage of them. Their lateral (sideways) movement should be excellent for this reason.

COACH'S CORNER

If you step on the center line, make sure that part of your foot stays on your side of the court. Otherwise you will be offside.

Middle hitters are useful attackers. As middle hitters, they hit a quick, low set, giving the other team little time to react. As hitters, middle players are useful for starting quick attacks and off-speed spikes to keep the other team off guard. In offensive moves, middle players are often the surprise playmakers.

Middle players practice their positions to find weak spots on the court.

These players take turns setting the ball to the front court.

Calling the Shot

Good offense demands good communication. Volleyball players use calls to communicate with teammates. Here are four offensive calls.

Calling for the ball is important to let your teammates know you will receive it and to put them in position to help you with the play. "Mine," "ball," or "I've got it" are examples. Players often call "over" during offensive moves to let their teammates know that the ball must go over on the next hit. This call keeps players from hitting the ball more than three times.

If you receive the ball while playing setter, you cannot hit it two times in a row. Call "setter out" to let your teammates know that someone else must do the set. "Help!" is also useful. If the ball is coming over the net and you see that the other team will not be able to make an attack, call "free" to let your team know that the ball is coming easily. Using these calls during offensive moves helps your team work together.

GLOSSARY

attack approach (uh TAK uh PROCH) — the movement of an attacker into position to attack

attack (uh TAK) — the main offensive move in volleyball

back overhead pass (BAK O ver HED PAS) — an overhead pass directed to a player behind the passer

dink (DINGK) — an off-speed attack; See "tip"

forearm pass (FAWR AHRM PAS) — the basic passing technique using the forearms as the contact area

hard-driven spike (HARD DRIV en SPYK) — the standard spike, very fast and forceful

jump set (JUMP SET) — a set performed by jumping up to meet the ball and contacting it with both hands at the forehead

off-speed spike (OFF-SPEED SPYK) — rather slow, or less forceful spike; a "dink" and "tip"

overhead pass (O ver HED PAS) — the basic passing technique using both hands and overhead motion

pass (PAS) — the act of moving the ball from one teammate to another

set (SET) — a pass that prepares the ball for the hitter to attack

setter (SET er) — the player responsible for setting the ball to the hitter

GLOSSARY

setter attack (SET er uh TAK) — a strategy in which the front court setter attacks instead of setting

spike (SPYK) — the attack move, performed by hitting the ball overhand over the net with a downward path

three-hits-and-over (THREE-HITS-AND-O ver) — the rule that a team may contact the ball only three times to send it over the net; also, a common technique in preparing for an attack

tip (TIP) — an off-speed attack; see "dink"

FURTHER READING

Find out more with these helpful books and information sites:

American Coaching Effectiveness Program, Rookie Coaches Volleyball Guide. Champagne, IL: Human Kinetics, 1993.

Howard, Robert E. *An Understanding of the Fundamental Techniques of Volleyball.* Needham Heights, MA: Allyn and Bacon, 1996.

Kluka, Darlene, and Dunn, Peter. *Volleyball.* Wm. C. Brown, 1996.

Neville, William S. *Coaching Volleyball Successfully.* New York: Leisure, 1990.

Vierra, Barbara, and Ferguson, Bonnie Jill. *Volleyball: Steps to Success.* Human Kinetics, 1996.

American Volleyball Coaches Association at
http://www.volleyball.org/avca/index.html

Complete worldwide source for volleyball information at
http://www.volleyball.org/
This site includes descriptions and ordering information for many new books and videos; also, many links.

Great links: http://users.aol.com/vballusa/index.htm

Online Volleyball Magazine subscription page at
http://www.volleyballmag.com/sub.htm

More volleyball information at http://www.volleyball.com

INDEX